THE CREATION OF ICONS
A Simple Guide for Iconography

Colette Maria Evans, Ph.D. & Maria Pente
FIRST EDITION

Cover Icon by Maria Pente

THE CREATION OF ICONS
A Simple Guide for Iconography

Colette Maria Evans, Ph.D. & Maria Pente
FIRST EDITION

Cover Icon by Maria Pente

This is Colette Maria Evans' personal experience learning from Maria Pente, a master iconographer, the techniques involved in creating traditional Icons. The demonstration images are Colette's first attempts at iconography, with expert guidance from Maria, who has been creating icons for over 30 years. Maria often corrected errors and set the foundation. In the background of some of the photos are icons Maria finished during the period Colette was studying with her. The only icons Colette created are the demonstration icons, accomplished with Maria's assistance. We wanted to make this book as realistic and practical as possible, so we kept the images raw and in the studio. I wish to thank JoEllen Collins for helping to edit this book. Also, deep gratitude and many thanks to my family and everyone who opened doorways making it possible for my extended stay in Patmos to study with Maria. Maria, thank you for sharing your gifts with the world.

Cover art work by Maria Pente
Book Design by Colette Maria Evans and Maria Pente
Photographs by Colette Maria Evans and Maria Pente
Published by Inspire LLC - Inspire Peace Print & Productions

First Edition

FOREWORD

THE ARTIST MARIA PENTE

Maria was born in Patmos, Greece, the blessed island of the Apocalypse. As soon as she found her artistic disposition, she researched ways to express her creativity, and finally specialized in the art of hagiography or iconography. Hagiography proved the most expressive way for her and simultaneously offered the opportunity to approach the religious and the spirituality contained in this art.

During her long creative course she studied the art of hagiography with the great hagiographer Vaggelis Theodorakis (1990) and the important hagiographer and art conservator Vaggelis Zournatzis (1992), where she specialized in the art of polished gold leaf.

It is important to point out some significant stages in her career. She held a personal exhibition (1995) at the Greek Orthodox Monastery of Saint John the Theologian of Patmos, for the anniversary of 1900 years from its establishment. She also took part in the group exhibition of the Holy Metropolis of Athens (2004). Furthermore, after the election of patriarch Vartholomeos, Maria was asked to create a series of icons and amulets, which were used as presents for his visits (1991-1992).

Above: Maria Pente, in her studio, Patmos, Dodecanese, Greece, 2018

Since 2007, she has had the unique experience of offering hagiography lessons for children and adolescents, under the auspices of Care and Family Support Center. Maria's icons are located at many private collections and churches, in her studio, located on the Island of Patmos, Dodecanese, Greece, in the 2018 Orthodox Patriarchate of Istanbul, also in the museum of the holy Monastery of Saint John the Theologian of Patmos, the Cave of Apocalypse of Patmos, the temples of Evagelistria at Kampos of Patmos, Theotokos of Grava of Patmos, St. Nektarios at Loukakia of Patmos, St. Platon at Epsimia of Patmos,

Theotokos Geranou of Patmos, St. John Prodromos at Skala of Patmos, Assumption of Mary at Agnanta of Arta, and St. John Prodromos at Neos Voutzas of Attiki. Her works for private collections are in several cities in Greece, Germany, USA, UK, Italy, France, Denmark, Australia, etc.

Right and Below: Icons Maria Pente completed during the time I was studying with her. Patmos, Greece

A BEGINNER'S PERSPECTIVE

COLETTE MARIA EVANS

Now that you have read about Maria's extensive background, mine is the opposite when it comes to iconography. I am new to the creation of icons. My love for icons started as a young girl, when I would sit in our small Greek Orthodox Church in Pocatello, Idaho, mesmerized by the icons displayed. My Greek heritage introduced me to their importance. I expanded my understanding and love of icons through my travels to places that are home to some of the most treasured icons, such as Jerusalem, Rome, Paris, Cyprus, and Greece. In the presence of icons, one can be deeply moved, blessed, and transformed. For me, the healing beauty represented in the softer versions of icons was what motivated me to want to learn iconography. I have some background in painting, mainly with landscapes and abstract oil painting. However, inspired by the transformative icons I have seen, I was ready to start to teach myself icon painting. I ordered a workbook, watched on-line videos, and prepared my first icon board, but I soon realized I needed the insight and wisdom of a master.

Knowing my love of icons, our mutual friends, Mike Robinson and Jo Le-Rose, introduced me to Maria Pente. Her work is striking, detailed, and filled with bright light. I had the opportunity to visit her in Patmos, Greece, over a five day period to watch her paint. I quickly realized that, in order to learn properly, I needed to have an extended stay to study with her. This led me to my journey to Patmos to create three icons. Maria is an amazingly brilliant teacher who creates transfixing icons and is an inspiring motivator. Here begins our journey.

As I was taking detailed notes and photos of the process, we felt it would be helpful to put this together from a beginner's perspective, showing the steps Maria taught and modeled for me. This book describes the day-by-day experience, over a two month period, when Maria taught and demonstrated indispensable tips for icon painting. She's the master: thus I am relaying steps which include ancient techniques and insights from her thirty years of experience. Some materials she has adapted for the longevity, transporting, and preserving of the icons. I have included the steps she shared for anyone wanting to learn or refine their technique. She paints quickly and with an expert's ease.

My first icon took over 20 hours to complete, consuming 1.5 to 2 hours per day until it was completed. This does not include board preparation time. We will follow the process Maria guided me through and the transformative experience of bringing out the light step-by-step.

Sometimes Maria would model a technique on one portion of the icon and then I would practice on the other half. She often corrected my mistakes. Having a teacher for guidance is the best approach for creating icons, because there are many nuances to the art. What I describe is Maria's process through the eyes of a beginner.

This book is broken into sections covering each of the three icons that I created while studying with Maria. Because my time was limited in Patmos, we touched on board preparation, but primarily focused on the steps necessary for painting. We will describe briefly board preparation, gold leaf, signing of the icon, and completion. I have included the details I found most helpful. Maria explained and modeled the process in such detail, that we hope this guide gives enough of a starting point to begin the exciting art of iconography.

Each section is presented in raw form, meaning that it includes my mistakes as well as successes. I learned through my mistakes and hopefully this helps shed light on the importance of proper board preparation, mixing the paints correctly, and an overall dedication to taking the proper time for each step. The board preparation, tracing of the icon, and gold leaf are shown in the first section. We then present each icon through a step-by-step process. Iconography is such a beautiful form of creation. Layer by layer the icons are brought to life. I hope you enjoy the masterful steps Maria shared with me that result in icons with much depth, color, and light.

CHAPTER 1

BOARD PREPARATION

Icon board preparation is an art in itself. Patience and practice are key. Each step, from board preparation to final signature, requires dedication to assure the correct steps are taken. Rushing, particularly for beginners, can result in mistakes. I am presenting a short version for initially preparing the board for painting, after the board has already been cut to size, designed, and sanded. This is a foundational step that must be done properly to assure a smooth working surface.

I arrived on Patmos with 'practice boards' which I prepared with gesso. The gesso technique was not up to standards, so for learning purposes, we continued with the board to see the outcome between a smooth and properly prepared board versus one that is less smooth. It is possible to see the rough texture showing through the gold leaf on the icon of Christ shown on page 16. The smoothness of the gold leaf, as a result of a properly prepared board, can be seen on the icon of Mary and Archangel Michael on pages 35 and 61 respectively.

Above and below: Maria prepared this icon board with muslin cotton layer and glue.

Traditional icon board preparation consists of adding the first layer of muslin cotton and then gesso layers. The cross image to the right shows Maria's work preparing the board first with muslin cotton and glue. If the icons are going to be transported a great deal and moved to various climates, Maria recommends an acrylic gesso to help assure safe travel, durability, and adaptability to climate changes, specifically humidity or dryness and heat or cold.

After the board has been prepared and sanded, glue is applied over the muslin cotton layer. There are many online videos demonstrating building icon boards and applying muslin cotton with glue and gesso. Maria has several boards she is working on at the same time. This assures that some are in the drying process while the others are ready for painting. She often uses driftwood. The surface must be very smooth. I used thin practice boards for ease of travel.

I have applied cotton to boards, using a hot plate to warm the glue, a time consuming process. Typically it takes one to three days for the cotton and glue to dry. For durability, Maria now uses a wood glue to apply the cotton. This, as well as an acrylic gesso, assures long-term stability in various climates and eliminates the need to heat the glue.

Applying the gesso was also something I experimented with at home. Without care the gesso can crack. What I learned from Maria is the essential need for an extremely smooth surface for painting. I found it difficult, so I suggest patience while sanding to get the boards completely smooth before painting. Mixing the appropriate consistency of gesso can be complicated, so acrylic gesso is preferred. There are many on-line resources for board making, glue and gesso mixing, or one can use already prepared glue and gesso. Once the artist has the gesso and glue, the following steps are taken for getting the gesso smooth enough for painting. The steps:

1. Glue cotton onto prepared board. Let dry 1-3 days, according to the climate. If it is humid, it will take much longer than in dry climates.

2. 1st layer gesso. Apply gesso using a spatula to make it smooth. Use acrylic gesso for long term durability. Let it dry two days.

3. 2nd layer gesso. Use a spatula to apply another layer. Make it as smooth as possible. Let dry two days.

4. 3rd layer gesso. Apply the final layer of gesso and let it dry two days.

Above: Cotton applied with glue using a hot plate to warm the glue.

Below: Gesso applied on boards. This was my first attempt at home prior to working with Maria.

5. Sand the gesso to create a very smooth surface.

6. The icon board is sanded with six different types of sandpaper. Sandpaper is available in various grits. The lower the grit number, the more coarse the sandpaper will be. The higher the number the less coarse it will be. The less coarse is necessary for the finish work. To properly prepare the board, it is important to use a sequence from coarse to fine sandpaper. The grit order follows. The icon painting surface needs to be extremely smooth with no rough areas. It is important to sand any imperfections, such as holes, or rough areas until the surface is completely smooth.

   o Use 120 grit sandpaper to sand the gesso covered board. One can use a hand held sanding block or place the sandpaper over a small block of wood to make the first step easier. Do not use an electric sander for any of these sanding steps.
   o Use 150 grit sandpaper by hand or with a hand held sanding block.
   o Use 180 grit sandpaper by hand.
   o Use 220 grit sandpaper by hand.
   o Use 320 grit sandpaper by hand.
   o Use 400 grit sandpaper by hand.

Below: Image of a finished board properly prepared for painting and gold leaf.

CHAPTER 2

THE IMAGE & GOLD LEAF

THE IMAGE

Selecting an appropriate image is a key beginning step. Maria selected three images for me to work on during my stay in Patmos. It is important that the first image is very basic. The painter can then gradually select more complex icons. I worked on three icons while in Patmos. I will describe the process Maria guided me through for each.

Icon 1 *Icon 2* *Icon 3*

The first step is selecting the icon to replicate. We have included a template at the end of this book for each of the three icons selected. The above photos are three of Maria's icons she selected as templates. These are beautiful, simple icons. They are fantastic for first efforts. Please see Chapter 6, page 83-85, for photographs of the icons we used as templates. Once the image has been selected, it is important to make a photocopy the size of the icon board. Clean the properly prepared icon board with a cotton ball and alcohol. Now it is time to transfer the image to the board. First, use a pencil to trace the image, placing tracing paper over the printed icon template. Then, place the tracing paper image over a carbon sheet to transfer the image to the board. It is possible to trace directly from the template to the board using carbon paper, but tracing paper is helpful when first learning. Make sure to trace the major lines. Around the eyes, only trace ONE line in-between the top and bottom lines that surround the eyes.

Look at the images on this page to see the heavy line on top of the eye and two faint lines on the bottom of the eye. The heavy line on top is correct. Do the same for the bottom part of the eye. Trace a line in-between the two faint lines, using a round tip tool. See image on the bottom left for the correct tool used for transferring the image using carbon paper.

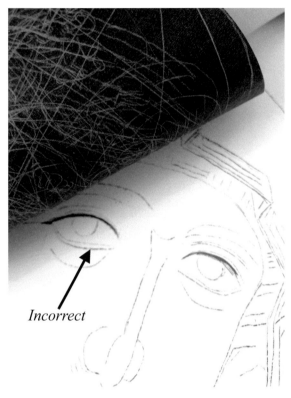

Incorrect

Left: The bottom two faint lines under the eyes on the image to the left are a mistake. Only one line is traced in-between these two faint lines; otherwise the eyes will be the wrong size.

Below: See the tracing below. The heavier line right below the eye is correct. It was drawn in-between the faint lines to make one heavier line.

Above: Tool used for transferring the image to the board.

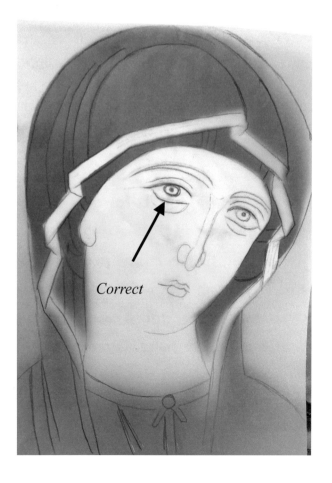

Correct

APPLYING THE GOLD LEAF

The importance of proper board preparation for the gesso and layers of glue is made evident when applying gold leaf. Again, it is essential to have an extremely smooth surface. The Icon of Christ is on a practice board I had prepared at home and brought with me to Patmos. The image to the right and those that follow in Chapter 3 demonstrate what can happen when the board is not prepared properly and when mixed metal gold leaf is used.

The second and third icons I made were prepared by using the gesso and sanding techniques recommended by Maria. Also, it is critical to use the proper gold leaf. The Icon of Christ was prepared using a mixed metal gold leaf. This type of gold leaf tends to tarnish and change color. The gold leaf best suited for icons consists of 22 or 23-karat gold. The type Maria uses is named Giusto Manetti, Firenze.

Once the icon image has been been traced, it is time to prepare it for gold leaf. Prepare the board by using a larger flat paintbrush to apply shellac. The shellac is made by mixing 1/3 portion fine granular rabbit glue and 2/3 93% alcohol. It is important to

Above: The lack of smoothness can be seen where gold leaf was applied.

Below: Materials needed for gold leaf application.

Read the labels for any of the substances and pigments used. Handle according to directions provided by the manufacture. Pigments, alcohol, shellac, varnish, glues, gesso and etc. all pose various health risks. Gloves and masks are recommended when handling pigments and when sanding.

mix the two together and let stand for two days before applying.

Using a flat paintbrush, apply shellac to the area of the icon where there will be gold leaf. There is a more advanced technique for applying gold leaf, but for the first icons, this is the simplest method. Apply the shellac and let dry for ten minutes. Once dry, sand by hand with 400 grit sandpaper. This process is repeated three times in total, sanding after each new layer of shellac. Shellac and glue for gold leaf can be purchased, but be sure to use white or clear shellac.

Once all three layers of shellac have been applied, paint on the glue. The glue is applied with very soft smooth brush strokes. DO NOT sand. Hold the board up to the light to see if it is dry. It typically takes 10 minutes. Apply three levels of glue, drying between each layer. DO NOT touch the glue to test for dryness. This will cause fingerprints to show in the gold leaf. Use a very soft brush stroke and very light layers of the glue. Once the third layer is dry, immediately apply the gold leaf, otherwise dust will get onto the board and cause bubbling or marks. With firm pressure, use a soft buffing tool (bottom right image on page 18) to pat down the gold leaf. Then, use the same buffing tool, to apply circular motions to further secure the gold leaf. The final step involves dipping a cotton ball in shellac to apply one thin layer over the gold leaf. This method of applying gold leaf is fairly easy, as long as the board is smooth, the shellac and glue have been applied properly, and the correct gold leaf is used.

Above: The sheen that can be seen on a very smooth surface. Check by visually checking if it is dry or not. Do NOT touch to test for dryness, otherwise fingerprints will be seen through the gold leaf.

Above: Flat brush needed for glue layers.

Maria applying the gold leaf. The image on the bottom right shows the soft tool used to make sure the gold leaf has bonded properly to the board. Maria prepared this with a soft velvet fabric over cotton and wood.

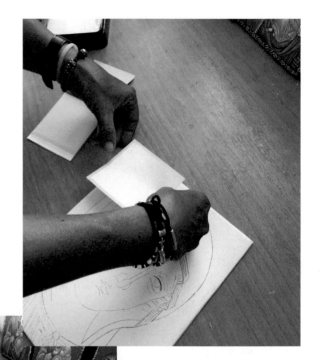

Below: Soft buffing tool for assuring the gold leaf has bonded to the board.

18

CHAPTER 3

ICON OF CHRIST

The first icon we worked on was an image of Christ. It is a very basic, less complex icon. Featuring mainly his face and beard, it provided an excellent starting point to learn the techniques used on the face.

MIXING OF THE PAINT

Mixing the paint is the most personal aspect of icon creating. Certain colors are traditional for many aspects of the icon, but it is the artist's choice for the desired tone. This is something that takes time to master. Maria expertly mixes colors very quickly. She often combined colors I would not have expected. Practicing is key.

Because proper paint mixing is the foundation for the entire icon, it is essential to take enough time to succeed. I had practiced at home, but watching Maria helped tremendously. Proper preparation requires choosing the correct pigments, preparing the egg mixture, and blending the pigments for the right colors. The pigments Maria used for the various colors will be presented throughout this book. They will be listed as they were used on the icons presented as samples. There is also a color guide in Chapter 6, pages 81 and 82. The color guide provides a general idea, but colors may not be exact due to fluctuation that can occur with photography, printing, and manufacturers labeling colors differently.

In addition to knowing the right pigments for the desired tone, proper egg preparation is also important. Egg combined with water is used to mix the pigments. The egg mixture that is used to mix the pigments and for painting areas of less light is made with one egg yolk, 1 teaspoon vinegar, and 1 teaspoon water. To prepare the egg mixture, separate the egg yolk from the egg white. Gently rinse the egg yolk with water. Break the membrane of the yolk and pour the mixture into a small container. Then add a teaspoon each of vinegar and water. Mix and let sit for 5 minutes for proper blending. Maria uses a plastic container with a thin, pointed, open lid to be able to squeeze out drops of egg mixture when necessary. Please note: when I use the word "egg" when talking about mixing the paints it means the "egg mixture."

The pigments are in dry form and are mixed directly prior to use, per color, layer, and light layers. Use caution when working with dry pigments, as handling instructions are recommended for each pigment type. Ordering the correct pigment color can be a challenge. The pigment names often vary in different countries. Please use the color guide at the end of this book as a starting point, but then choose pigments based on the colors and tones desired for the chosen icon.

Maria mixes the paint as she works. She uses a small plastic palette with six different areas and keeps the current pigments while working. In other words, if she is painting the robe or face, she keeps the previous light layers on the palette in case touch up work is necessary. This is often why she works in continuous blocks of time: otherwise the paints dry. She mixes the pigments on the palette first and then uses a glass table surface to further mix the shades as needed. This process will make more sense as I describe the process for each of the three icons.

THE ROBE

The first step for painting occurs only after the gold leaf has been applied. If there is a halo, it must be created before painting other parts of the icon. The creation of a halo is shown in Chapter 5, page 61. It is quite an amazing process. Halos require a lot of practice to master the technique. The painter needs to try making halos on scratch paper to be able to master the technique. If there is no halo, the first item to paint is the robe. The steps are described as they were completed. Work on one color of the robe at a time and save the paint in the palette for color comparison if corrections are needed.

Below: Sample to demonstrate the thick lines and small brush strokes for the light layers on the red robe.

Red Part of the Robe

Base color: red + blue. The main color is red with a very small amount of blue. The small amount of blue added to the red makes a deeper color for the base.

The first step is to prepare the paint for the main base color of the robe. We started with the red portion of the robe. In this case, it is made with red, blue, and egg (approximately a little less than 1/4 teaspoon of egg mixture and just a small amount of pigment) to create the base color. Because Maria is a pro at this, she does not need to measure, but just automatically knows the right consistency and color tone. It takes practice to get the desired color and texture. It needs to be smooth and not too runny. For the base, the paint must be a solid color when painted. If too much egg is used, it will be too transparent.

Color tones are the personal choice of the icon painter. The entire red portion of the robe is covered with the base color, without additional egg. This makes a solid base color. Light layers are then painted on the base layer. Apply the first layer, allow it to dry and then apply a second layer. Once the robe has been painted with two layers, the pencil lines of the robe can be difficult to see. The lines can be re-drawn by hand or traced using tracing paper and a round tip tool to give faint lines. Make sure each layer is dry. It does not take long to dry, but rushing the process with it still wet causes pulling off the paint rather than adding another layer. The base needs to be a solid color with no white showing through.

Lines of the Robe

The next step is preparing the paint for the lines of the robe. The lines are painted with strong brush strokes. A darker shade of paint is used for the lines. This is created by using the base color of the robe and adding additional pigment.

Line color: darker red (the base color) + blue + more blue. The base color is used and then more blue pigment is added until the desired shade of deep red is achieved. The lines for the robe are painted with smooth, bold, long strokes. All of the lines on the red part of the robe are painted, including the neckline, as on the original icon.

Light Layers

Adding layers of light builds the icon into a beautiful piece of work. Each layer requires care, precision, and mixing the desired color. Light layers are created using lines, working out from the main anchor line. The images of Christ's robe on pages 20 and 23, show how the lines are painted in a multidirectional fashion. The main line directs the other crossing lines. The major lines are painted with pure color and then egg is added to blend and add directional lines. This will be made more clear in the icon of Mary where we show photos of the lines.

Above: Directional lines that will be used throughout the icon painting process. Right: Glass is used for the mixing palette so colors can be easily seen when mixed with egg. This allows for easier mixing to get the desired degree of transparency.

Maria uses a table covered in glass to be able to mix her paint with additional egg. This is very practical, easy to clean, and helps the process immensely. She can put egg directly on the glass, mix with the colors, and for touch-up work add pigment when necessary.

1st layer of light: red + a little orange + a little white. The first layer of light is added in broader brush strokes and creates the new base for further layers of light. First paint in the area that needs more light with pure color. The next step is to add egg to the color to blend. In some areas, use egg only to move the color and blend it with the other layers.

2nd layer of light: red + orange + white + a little yellow. The second layer of light is added with thinner brush strokes than were used on the previous layer of light. These lines cover the area that needs to be a lighter color when compared to the first layer. Keep the template icon as a guide. Smooth, long brush strokes are used.

3rd layer of light: red + orange + white + gold ochre + white. For each subsequent layer add long lines with pure color, or where it needs light, and then use shorter directional lines with pure color mixed with additional egg. Sometimes only the egg mixture is used to blend the colors. In most cases, though, working from the base color, more of the lighter pigments and/or a bit of white are added to the previous light color to make the mixed paint lighter for the next light layer. This takes practice to determine, so experimentation with the various pigment mixtures is encouraged. The appropriate formulation depends on the color being used and the desired shade. Adding white changes the tone and can be difficult to work with, so it is important to only use a small amount of white when choosing it as the method to lighten the color. Also, save the base, lines, and light layer colors when working. Therefore, if mistakes are made, the color is already ready to be used without having to mix new paint. If the paint has already dried, that is okay; it can be used to color match when mixing new paint. Because the paint dries quickly, Maria works in large blocks of time. For example, she paints each day for several hours.

Blue Part of the Robe

Base color: blue + green. Mix the green and blue pigment with egg to make a nice smooth tempura paint. Paint the entire surface of the blue part of the robe. Approximately two or three layers of paint will be necessary. Be sure to let each layer dry before adding the next layer. If it is wet, it will pull off the paint, rather than cover the area. The base layer is the most opaque layer. The paint needs to be applied so that no white can be seen though the paint.

Above: Pigments for the blue part of the robe.

Lines of the Robe

Line color: blue + green + black. This will be darker than the base color. Paint the lines in bold, smooth strokes. Use the original image to determine the size, length, and width of the lines. The cleaner the lines, the stronger the icon will appear.

Light Layers

1st layer of light: base color + white. Use this color for the first layer of light. Make sure to use long, smooth brush strokes. To create lower light, which means it appears slightly darker, add more pigment or egg to the paint. Two layers of each light layer is typically enough.

2nd layer of light: base color + more white. The second layer of light will be added with thinner brush strokes. The image to the right shows the lines, which are the darkest blue; then the 1st, 2nd, and 3rd layers of light can be seen clearly and show how typically thinner lines are used for subsequent layers. Large areas may be covered with the lighter colors, but thinner strokes are used. This gives more dimension to the icon.

3rd layer of light: 2nd light + more white. With each layer of light, first use the main color without adding additional egg. Once that has been applied, typically two or three times, mix with egg to blend with the base or other light layers. Apply two layers of each light layer color.

Above: Lines & light layers on the blue rope. Pay close attention to the thin lines and directional changes of the brush strokes.

Right: Base color for face. Below: The base color applied to the entire face and neck.

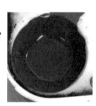

THE FACE

Once the robe is complete, it is now time to paint the face. The first part of the face is the base layer. The base color is used to cover the entire face, including the beard for this particular icon.

Base Layer

Pigments: dark red + red + fresco green + ochre + yellow. Cover everything on the base layer of the face with the base color. Paint the first layer, let it dry and then add the second

layer. It will be difficult to see the pencil lines on the face. Use tracing paper and a round tipped tool to trace major lines. Do not trace the fine lines, only one line above and below the eyes in addition to the heaviest lines on the face.

Lines for Face and Beard

Line color: dark red (like brown) + black. Use smooth brush lines to paint the lines on the face. For the beard and mustache, add some extra egg to make the lines less dark. Soft brush strokes are necessary.

The hair is dark brown, using the same color as the lines. The eyes are outlined with one line. The nose, mouth, and eyes have very clean, smooth lines. Do not paint the upper mouth line. The eyebrows, hair, and eyes are filled in completely with two layers of paint. Dry between each layer. For the beard and mustache, more egg is added to make thinner lines and more transparent paint. The eyes must be ROUND in shape. Add mainly the egg mixture to make it very light around the eyes and above eyebrows (see the image at the top right of this page).

Above: Lines on the face, beard, and light brown above the eyes and eyebrows. First brush strokes for the 1st light layer. Below: Pigments used for the 1st light layer and cross patterns used for light layers on the face.

Light Layers

1st layer of light: red cadmium + yellow cadmium. Apply the first light lines above the eye brows, on the forehead, nose, under eyes, and then use eggs to blend on the face. Use similar brush strokes as more layers are applied.

The first layer of light is quite a bright orange color. The light is added in lines, first in one direction, sometimes slightly arching to follow the main lines, then crossing lines, creating a crossing pattern. The fine detail is shown in the images to the right. Use a cross pattern with these lines to fill in the area. Do not fill in

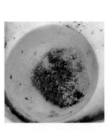

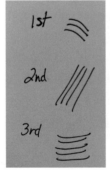

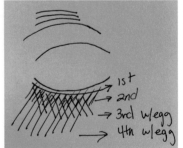

Above: Completed 1st light layer.
Below: Application of the 2nd light layer.

the dark areas. Those are the shadow areas, so the base color must be visible. Study the images for details. Cross patterns take practice to determine the impact they have on subsequent layers. Careful application of the layers creates the depth and beauty of the icon. Seven layers are often used for each light layer.

2nd layer of light: bright red + yellow + more yellow. This color must be lighter than the first light layer. Maria keeps the mixing trays with the previous colors. Even if the paint dries, it can be used to match the color when mixing new paints. Use the second light color where it needs the most light. Then add a layer with a little color and egg. The egg mixture is sometimes used without pigment, particularly on the edges near the base color, which creates the appearance of a shadow. Using only egg moves the color and blends the layers together.

Again, do not paint over the base color that is starting to look like a shadow. Each light layer may be blended slightly with egg when getting near to the base color, but where there is the darkest shadow, the color remains the base color.

Egg is used to blend the colors. Maria applies extra egg directly to the glass; therefore she can mix a little color with additional egg, or use just egg depending upon what is needed. Continue to use the crossing pattern. For the eyes, paint following the lines of the eyes and use very short thin lines and then add longer lines with egg. Use a thin paint brush for fine lines.

3rd layer of light: red + yellow + more yellow + gold ochre. For the third layer of light, cross patterns are used. Follow the main lines and use pure color where you need the most light. Then use egg to blend the light with longer, thin lines. Around the eyes thin short lines are painted at an angle to the eye contour. Continue to use and practice with the cross patterns. Make sure to blend well with egg mixed with color.

Right: Face with 3rd light layer. Left: Gold ochre and yellow pigments used for subsequent light layer. Bottom Right: 4th light layer.

4th layer of light: red + yellow + more yellow + gold ochre. The same steps are used, but less area is covered with the pure color. Egg is added to blend and make the color a little more transparent where there is less light. Cover the face using directional lines in a crossing pattern. The lines follow the main dark lines of the face and then work outward from that point by mixing egg with a bit of color and longer lines. Only egg is then used with long thin lines to blend the layers. Egg makes the finish smoother. Each light layer requires several layers of painting. Thin brush strokes are used to apply the paint, using the cross patterns.

5th layer of light: orange + yellow + gold ochre + a little white. The same process is repeated. Make sure to use crossing lines and blending methods. The lines initially follow above the eyebrow, but only in the middle, not the entire length, of the eyebrow. The lines are placed above the eye, below the eye, on and around the left side of the nose, on both sides of the bottom lip, and on the ear lobes. Use very thin brush strokes with a paintbrush size #1 or #2, for smaller lines a #0. Paintbrushes are usually numbered according to size with #0 - 000 being very small. Higher numbers indicate thicker brushes. The size is typically indicated on the handle of the brush.

Above: 5th light layer.
Left: 6th light layer.

6th layer of light: yellow + gold ochre + white. Use the same process and build the depth of the light. For each light layer, cover less area and use more egg mixture to blend with the other layers. Lines of pure color are painted in the areas with highest light. This process takes practice. Thin brush strokes are used. The areas above the eyes, under the eyes, nose, and any area with the most light require very fine short lines, except along the major lines of the face. Use the major lines as a guide and then build light using the short crossing patterns. Again, do not add light to the areas of shadow which are still in the original base color. A small amount of egg, with a bit of color, can be used when painting closer to the shadow areas, but do not cover those areas, such as on the side of the neck, between the eyes and eye brows, under the chin, and any other shadow areas.

27

7th layer of light: yellow + white + gold ochre. This color will be lighter again than the previous layers. Because it has white, it is harder to work with and must be applied with thin lines and then blended with egg as needed. Do not use excess paint: the white tone becomes more complicated and difficult to blend properly. Blend and smooth out each area, using additional egg mixture as needed. Cross layers are used for blending. For the final touches, the egg mixture will be used without adding pigment.

Right: Observe the cross patterns used for the 7th light layer as shown in the image. The lines are very thin and gradually get thinner and longer, but shorter thin lines are used under the eyes, on the forehead, and around the mouth.

Final Face Layer

The final layer of the face is painted using six steps. *Color: white - use a 00 paintbrush for lines.* Place lines as follow (see image):

Below: Lines for the 8th light layer

1. Eyes - three lines above eyebrow just above center (left eye) longer for (right eye). When referring to left and right, it is left and right as the image is viewed by the reader.

2. Under Eyes - three lines on the outside and inside of the left eye, four on the inside of the right eye, and three lines on the outside of the right eye. The farthest line to the left of the right eye extends past the nose.

3. Forehead - five or six lines on the forehead.

4. Nose - Two lines on the nose and three lines around the left nose nostril.

5. Ears, Lip, and Mouth - One line and two on lower lip.

6. Neck - Three lines (upper), one longer line and one shorter (middle), and three lines bottom.

FINAL TOUCHES AND BASE FOR EYES

Now, with a zero brush, *mix white + egg + little water (1 drop)*, and go over lines using the same techniques with the cross patterns used earlier. A very small amount of yellowish orange may be needed to smooth out areas that need blending once the white/egg/water mix has been painted. It must be smooth and finely blended.

Use a *dark, bright orange* and add a line above the upper eye lid and then add one more line with *yellow*. The image to the right shows this clearly above both eyes.

The upper lip is painted with *red*. The bottom lip is painted with a *bit of yellow + orange + red* then take *white* to paint over the bottom lip.

Above: Blending of white lines, adding yellow to blend lines if necessary, and yellow/orange lines around the eyes. Left: Lips as painted with layers of color.

30

The Base for Eyes

The following six steps are used for the base of the eyes:

1. The iris of the eyes are painted with a *dark bright orange*.

2. *Black* is used for the pupil.

3. *Dark red brown + dark brown ochre* is used for the next layer of the iris.

4. *Orange + red + yellow* is used for the third layer of the iris.

5. Then *brown + more egg* is used to go over the iris again, but it is applied very lightly.

6. *Dark brown* is used to paint a very thin line around the iris and to make the pupil darker if necessary.

Final Lines - For hair and Face

1. *Lines: egg + dark red (rust) + a little brown + black.* Use a #00 paintbrush or longer zero to line hair, line eyebrows, add a very fine line above eyes, and then add lines to the beard. Go around the hair, the neck, and face.

2. Pure black is used only around the face, hair, and top line of eyes.

3. *Brown + black.* Paint over and below eyebrows and thin lines on beard.

Above: The eyes are painted using layers of different colors for the iris and black for the pupil. Below: Final lines have been added to the hair and face.

31

THE HAIR

Base Color

Brown (same color as face lines). The base for the hair is painted at the same time and using the same color as the lines of the face. The entire hair area is painted and will be completely covered. This is only for the hair, not for the beard. Note how in the image below, some of the base color of the face can be seen showing under the beard.

1st Layer of Light

Brown + dark red (rust). Follow lines as per original icon, either by hand or trace onto the icon with a round tip tool and tracing paper. Paint the lines using long smooth brush strokes.

2nd Layer of Light

Orange + ochre + red. One, two, or three lines are painted. These lines are painted in-between the 1st light layer lines or on top to give the added light and color desired.

Hairline Part

Black + brown. With black and brown mix paint the hairline part and fine hair lines as needed.

Right: Hair painted with layers of light.

THE EYES

The final step to complete the icon before signing is the final touches to the eyes. The eyes bring the icon to life.

The Eyes

Blue + white. Use a #000 paintbrush. Paint the outside (left side) without egg (pure paint) and inside with paint and egg, then underneath the iris with one very thin line.

Only white. Using a #000 paintbrush, paint the outside (left side) without egg, with only white and a thin line under, then use a bit of color but mainly egg on the right side. This is repeated twice. Then repeat the entire process. Using white only, repeat up to four times, to get the desired finished look.

Above: First layer of blue around the iris, building the whites of the eyes. Below: The white added to make the whites of the eyes more balanced and bright.

33

SIGNING

Take time to look at the icon from a distance and up close and fix anything that needs fixing. Once this is completed, the icon is ready to be framed with a border (if desired), named, and signed. Before signing, the icon may get a border. We used a *rust* acrylic paint, to paint lines around the icon, including the sides, top, and bottom. The name can then be painted on the icon. The name is who the icon represents and is typically shown on the icon template. Use red to write the name on the top right and left. The artist now uses *white* to sign his or her name, the date, and location on the bottom right of the icon. The icon must dry for two months before varnishing. Maria uses a clear varnish made with alcohol and mastic. She uses 1/3 mastic and 2/3 98% alcohol. A varnish suitable for egg tempura paint may also be used instead.

Right: Finished icon of Christ.

CHAPTER 4

ICON OF MARY

THE FOUNDATION

We are now going to present the step-by-step process of painting Mary. Again, Maria selected this icon based on the simplistic beauty for first time icon painters.

THE ROBE, GOWN, AND HEADDRESS

Base Colors

Left: The paint used for the base colors. Below: Note the opaqueness of the base colors once two layers have been applied.

The robe is painted by first painting the base colors for both the red and blue parts of the robe, gown, and headdress.

Red: bright red + dark red OR bright red + blue. Both combinations make the same color. Cover the entire robe in two layers of this color using a larger brush and smooth brush strokes. As with the previous icon, the base color needs to be the most solid of colors. No white should show through the paint.

Dress/headdress: green + blue. Paint the dress and headdress with blue, covering completely with two layers of paint.

Once two or three layers of the base color have been applied to the robe/dress, it will be difficult to see the lines. Trace over tracing paper with a round tipped tool or draw by hand the lines. Tracing is the best way to assure clean lines. With much practice, the lines may then be drawn free hand.

Right: This image depicts how tracing paper can be used to mark soft lines on the opaque base layer. This image shows tracing paper, with pencil lines, placed on top of the icon image. A round tip tool is used to trace over the pencil lines. This results in light marks on the opaque base layer to show where lines need to be painted.

Lines on the Robe

Red + blue + more blue. This color will be darker than the base color. Paint the lines with smooth, strong brush strokes. Then use a bit of egg to cover broader areas where there is more shadow.

Above: Sample of lines and then shadow (small horizontal and vertical lines next to the dominant lines) applied to the robe. Right from top to bottom: Lines and then close up of vertical and horizontal lines that make the appearance of shadow.

Light Layers

1st layer of light: red + a little blue (less blue than base color). Paint with pure color and then use egg to mix for lighter color for blending and the longer lines which create light.

Above, right, and below: Light layers on the red robe showing highlighted areas, crossing patterns, and long lines.

2nd light layer: red + a little orange. Continue the same process with the 2nd light layer color in the areas with the most light and then add egg to blend. Use lines to give dimension as shown in the photos on this and the previous page.

  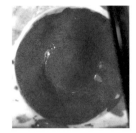 

Above: Pigments, mixed colors, and palette. Below: Image of lines, light layers, and detailed lines in a crossing pattern.

3rd layer of light: red + orange + white. Use the previous light color and then add a bit of white. This is used in the areas of highest light without adding extra egg mixture. The highest light areas are painted with pure color to make the color stronger. Then use egg with color or just the egg alone to blend into the other areas.

The Band of the Robe

Cover the band around the robe in orange.

Above: Bright orange is used for the band.

Below: Third light layer and band.

Blue on the Headdress and Dress

Lines on the blue headdress and dress: blue + black + a little green (darker than base color). Paint the lines using the dark line color. The lines are painted darker than the base color. Paint the lines in smooth, clear paint strokes. If the lines cannot be seen, use tracing paper, as described previously, to indicate where the lines need to be painted.

1st layer of light: green + blue + a little white. Paint the light areas with pure paint and then blend with egg. This may require covering a larger area than expected. Basically cover every area that has light, but do not paint over the shadow areas. Use stronger lines where there is the most light. Paint using small thin lines and then with egg and a bit of paint for the longer lines which will result in blending of the colors.

Left: Blue pigments used for the 1st layer of light. Above: 1st light layer on the headdress and dress.

41

2nd layer of light: 1st layer of light + more white. Again, using thin brush strokes, go over the lightest areas. Use egg to blend into the other layers. Make sure to use thin lines, but apply broader lines in the areas of more light. This layer typically requires two applications.

Below: 2nd light layer on blue headdress and dress.

3rd layer of light: 2nd layer of light + white. Using fine brush lines, highlight the areas with the most light. Use fine details to make the shape of the headdress and dress pronounced (see images on this page). Blend with egg to mix with the other layers. Keep the paint in the palette from the previous layers in order to make corrections as necessary. The highlights in the image to the right are done by adding a bit more white to the 3rd layer of light. This can be done by mixing directly on the glass palette. Add small lines or dots for highlighting.

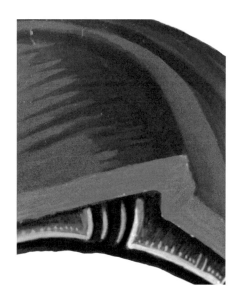

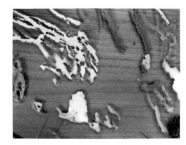

Left: The palette with previous layers of light and glass table for mixing extra white for the fine details. Above: Fine details added to the headdress.

Above and right: 3rd layer of light with one layer of paint and prior to adding fine details.

The Band of the Robe

The lines: cadmium red. Use a thin paintbrush to paint the outside lines of the band. One on the bottom and one on the top. Maria recommends a #1 paintbrush that has a longer tip.

The light layer: yellow + gold ochre. Using a thin, longer bristled paintbrush and bracing tool, paint the lines. They need to be painted twice to create a strong color. Do not mix with additional egg. At this point, draw the additional decorations on the robe. Save the red from the lines for any touch up work that is necessary. The glory (top center of robe in the image to the right) is also painted at this time. Use tracing paper if necessary or paint by free hand.

Above and right: Paint brush, bracing tool, pigments, and colors used for the band of the robe. Below: The glory and band of the robe.

THE FACE

Base Layer

Base layer: red (light) + dark red + green (fresco) + ochre + yellow. Paint the face and neck. Cover it with two to three layers, drying between layers. We used a #8 paintbrush. Of course this may be different based on the icon size. This icon is approximately 8 x 11 inches. The surface needs to be covered smoothly and completely. Make sure it is dry between each coat of paint.

The Lines of the Face

Once you have painted the face with the base color it may be difficult to see the lines of the face. If so, use the tracing paper with a round tipped tool to trace the lines onto the face. It leaves a small indentation in order to see where the lines need to be painted.

Line paint: base color + dark red. Paint the lines on the face. Use clean, strong, smooth brush strokes that thin to a point around the edge of the eye (see image to the right). Do not close the eye on the inside, but leave a small space between the two lines. Paint the right side line of the nose and bottom lines of the mouth. Fill in the eyebrows. Paint the circle of the iris and pupil, let dry, and then add red around the pupil of the eyes.

Above: Lines painted on the face. Please see the fine lines that come to a point around the eyes and mouth. Also, do not close the lines on the inside of the eyes.

45

1st layer of light: cadmium red + dark cadmium yellow + gold ochre + dab of water + egg. Apply the first layer of light by following the main lines where light is needed. For example, paint above the left eyebrow (as viewed by the reader) a small line to the middle left side. For the cheek, paint under the eye, but below the shadow area. Do the same for the neck, nose, and above the eyes. Paint is then applied using thin directional brush strokes as described for the previous icon. The areas that require the most light are painted with full color, a dab of water, and tiny bit of egg. A "dab" of water is created by dipping only the tip of the paintbrush in water, wiping it onto the glass table, then adding paint and a little egg. Paint the areas with less light with a mixture of egg, color, and a dab of water, then use only egg to blend the layers. Always keep the base color available for blending. This image is not quite finished: notice the base color still visible under some of the cross patterns. The areas of greatest shadow will remain the base color. Check the color as it dries. The color may need to be stronger. We adjusted the color, by adding less egg, for the image on the second light layer. The base layer is to be covered completely with color in the areas with the most light. It must be smooth and consistent. Do not paint over the areas with the darkest shadows. Compare the image of 1st layer of light and the 2nd layer of light. Use this same type of comparison to make sure it is covered properly. These layers are crucial to the overall result of the icon. Maria recommended using a #1 and #2 paintbrush, depending upon the size of the icon.

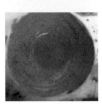

Above: Pigments and 1st layer of light color.

Below: 1st layer of light applied over base layer.

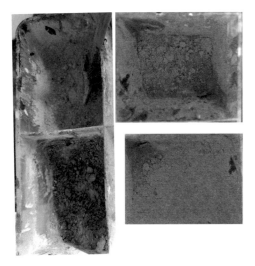

Above: Pigments used for 2nd light layer. Below: 2nd layer of light applied over base layer.

2nd layer of light: orange + a little red + yellow + gold ochre + a dab of water. Use the same crossing patterns with long thin light brush strokes to cover the lightest areas. Use the glass table to mix the color, with a dab of water and egg for the right consistency and level of color. When painting near the edge of the areas that are still the base color, use a little color with egg, and then only egg. If necessary, blend using the base color and 1st light color. At this point, it is important to correct any errors, like shading and softening sharp edges that are not blended enough. Notice the left side of the mouth. A softer blending of color makes the appearance of a small smile. Also on the chin, the line is softer than in the previous light layer.

Remember to use soft, light brush strokes. The first layers of light have longer lines with more color, and then gradually use shorter lines with full color. Always imagine what the next layer will be, so make sure to prepare the layer in anticipation of the next light.

These first layers of light are very important for building the foundation for the face. If done correctly, it will result in a well blended and very smooth face. These steps require patience and time. There are several layers painted with cross patterns of each layer of light. For example, there are at least seven layers of cross patterns used to complete the 2nd light layer.

3rd layer of light: orange + dark cadmium yellow + gold ochre. A dab of water with color and a little egg is used for this layer. The same principle is used for each additional light layer. Make sure each layer offers a gradual transition from the previous light layer. This is done by covering less of the previous layer. Only egg or egg with a little bit of color is used to blend the layers together. Each light layer requires several layers, using the same color with different directional patterns as previously described.

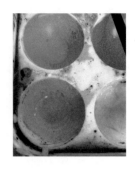

Above: Colors for the first three layers of light. Below: 3rd layer of light.

4th layer of light: a little third layer of light + yellow + gold ochre. For this layer, Maria used a little bit of the third layer of light, combining it with yellow, and gold ochre. A dab of water and egg is used to create the softer color. Take a close look at the image to the right and notice the length of the lines covering the highest area of light. The layers are then covered in a crossing pattern to create a smooth, more even light layer.

Above: (Left) Close-up image of 4th layer of light. (Right) First lines for the 4th layer of light. Below: (Left) 4th layer of light not yet complete. (Right) Completed 4th layer of light.

5th layer of light: yellow + gold ochre. Always keep the previous light color in the mixing palette to compare the new light layer. Be sure to dab the brush in water and add a bit more egg to the glass table for mixing. Mixing color with a drop of egg and dab of water creates a softer color for this particular icon. This layer of light requires just a bit of egg for the main areas of color, then only egg for the sides with the lower levels of light. Do not cover the base face color that is in the shadow with any egg or additional color. It may only be necessary in areas around the mouth, nose, or eyes to soften those areas. Pay attention to the mouth, nose, chin, and around the eyes on the image below to see the soft blending and smoothness.

Above: Colors for the 4th and 5th layers of light. Right: 5th layer of light.

6th layer of light: yellow + white + little gold ochre. Keep the previous light color in the mixing palette to compare with the new lighter layer. The degree of lightness is a personal choice, but for beginning icon painting it is easier to use the colors recommended by Maria. When starting to paint, dab the brush in water and add a bit more egg to the glass table for mixing.

When painting the face for this particular icon, mix color with a drop of egg and dab of water in order to create smooth, soft features. This is of increasing importance for the highest areas of light on the face. Paint with lines, again crossing several times until the color is right. Then use egg only, maybe a dab of color, to cover the larger surface of the face to blend the colors. All layers, but particularly this layer, need to be a very smooth blending of the lines. Adding the dab of water makes it so the paint will not crack, and it softens the colors.

Paint layer over layer of crossing lines, until the icon is the desired lightness. Always paint the layer of light in preparation for the next light layer. The painter must paint in anticipation of the next light layer.

Right and below: Finished 6th layer of light (the image on the left appears lighter due to it being a close-up image). Pay special attention to smooth and soft transitions around the eyes, nose, mouth, and sides of face.

Left: Titanium white. Right: (Upper) White lines for the most light. (Lower) Starting to blend the lines.

7th layer of light: titanium white. This is an essential layer of light, defined by the degree to which the previous layers of light were blended together and work as one. This layer is with white only, using a long #1 paintbrush. Maria uses titanium white.

The color is mixed in the standard way with egg. Then put a little color on the glass table to mix with a dab of water and egg. Use just a dab of water and egg for the lines. Once the lines are painted, use a tiny bit of color with egg to blend the lines with the previous layers. There are different ways to create the lines around the eyes and forehead. They can be done as shown on the image to the right (top). It depends on the icon being painted and the type of effect wanted with the light layer. The white line placement is different for this icon than on the icon of Christ.

Start blending with egg and just a dab of color, but first add softer white lines between the white lines. Repeat with longer lines of egg and a dab of color to blend the layers. There are several layers of mainly egg and a little color. Work slowly with this layer of light. Working with white can be a bit more difficult than with the other colors. Maria recommended that the painter needs to

take it slowly and have patience. For this layer, she demonstrated the technique by applying the first lines and then blending the lines with the other smaller lines painted in-between the first lines.

Of special note is the care necessary for each layer. These are very fine, thin lines, creating the effect of solid color, but with a result of becoming much more alive and vibrant. Patience is as important as well as using soft brush strokes. I pushed too hard with the paint brush a few times which created bare spots. Also, sometimes small hairs or dust particles can appear on the icon. If this occurs, try to remove them with a soft dry paint brush: take care not to damage the layers of paint.

Below: The fine white lines are blended using thinner white lines between the major white lines. Right: The resulting smoothness of the 7th layer if each previous layer and the final layer are completed with care.

THE LINES, IRIS, AND FOUNDATION FOR THE EYES

The Lines

Major lines (dark brown): sienna brown + a little black. Using brown, paint all the brown lines around the face, nose, eyes, mouth, and neck. This includes all the lines that were previously painted brown, except for the eyebrows. Only paint a thin line along the lower part of the eyebrow. Using egg to mix with the color, fill in the eyebrow.

Minor lines (very dark brown): sienna brown + a little more black. Paint the lines above and below the eyes. Paint a line around the iris of the eyes.

Pupil and Iris

Black. Paint the pupil, the upper eyelid line and the outline of the iris. Only paint

Below: Lines around the eye, nose, and eyebrow and finished iris and pupil.

the line on the top of the eye in black. Do not close the lines on the inside of the eye. A gap between the black upper line and brown lower line can be seen in the above image.

The Iris. Two colors are used. First, mix cadmium red with lots of egg and paint the iris, but do not cover the black line surrounding the iris and do not cover the pupil. Then mix ochre or dark yellow ochre with lots of egg and paint over the iris again. The color tone and number of layers depend on the color desired for the iris. The iris is painted using small lines directed from the outside line to the pupil. Let dry and mix egg with the colors to create the eye color desired. The eyes are to be done by feeling what tone of color is right for the icon. Each painter may have a slightly different preference for tone and brightness.

THE LIPS

Upper Lip

Red cadmium. Paint the upper lip, using the strong red cadmium. Add a little of dark sienna to the red cadmium and paint the bottom of the upper lip. Use extra egg to do this, so it blends smoothy.

Bottom Lip

Red cadmium + white. The bottom lip is painted with a mixture of red cadmium and a little white. Then mix a lighter pink with the *cadmium red, yellow,* and *white.* Use this to paint the lower lip mixed with extra egg.

Using extra *white,* with the *pink* already mixed, paint highlights on the lower lip. Always have a little base color prepared, as this is necessary to blend any areas where needed. Notice the sides of the upper lip and how they have been blended.

Above: Colors for the lips are mixed directly on the glass working surface. Below: Finished upper and lower lip.

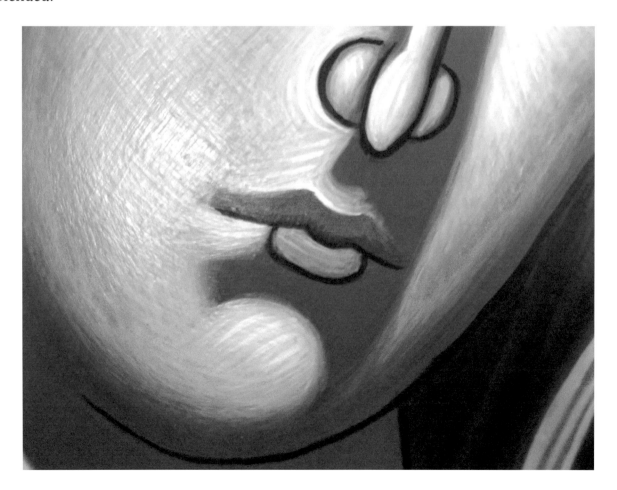

THE EYES

The last step is the eyes. It is quite amazing to watch the eyes come to life. I will present the three step process Maria outlined.

Above: Blues used for the eyes and sample of how the colors are mixed on the glass working surface. Below: Finished eyes.

1. *First color: bright blue + slightly darker blue + white.* Fill in the right side of both eyes. This is the right side as the painter views the icon. The full color will only be on the right side and slightly under the iris. Mix the color with additional egg to fill in the rest of the area. Let dry and repeat one or two additional times. Work slowly when painting the eyes. The color changes when it dries, so take the time to see how many layers are needed. Remember to keep the base color (the original base color for the face) to use if necessary for blending. Notice on the the left side of the white of the eyes, some of the base color can still be seen.

2. *Second color: Mix the 1st layer color with more white.* Using the same idea, start on the right side with full color and then mix with additional egg for the rest of the area. Let dry and repeat one or two additional times. Use egg to blend and add a little color.

3. *Third color: White.* Paint a very small area to the right side and under of the iris. Use egg to blend the colors. Repeat this process until the desired brightness has been achieved. Remember that the color changes as it dries. Do not rush the process.

FINAL TOUCHES

Once the eyes have been painted, look over the entire icon to see if there is anything that needs to be corrected or adjusted. It is best to let the icon dry, in order to see the final colors before making any changes.

FRAMING, NAMING, AND SIGNING

Use *red* to write the name on the top left and top right of the icon. *White* is used to sign the icon on the bottom right. The next step involves framing the icon with a painted edge. This will be the color of your choice that helps to highlight the icon. We used an acrylic paint, mixed with additional pigment to get the color desired. Maria made the lines for the icon to assure they were straight. This is something I will be practicing at home, before applying to my finished icons. Maria uses her supporting stick to make the lines straight. Turn the icon on its side to assist in making very clean, straight lines. The next step is to finish painting the sides of the board.

Clockwise (from top left): Red and white used for naming and signing were mixed directly on the glass working surface. Maria using her supporting stick as a bracing tool to paint the framing lines around the icon. The icon is turned on its side for painting the framing lines on each side.

Below: Finished icon of Mary.

CHAPTER 5
ICON OF ARCHANGEL MICHAEL
THE FOUNDATION OF THE ICON

The icon we selected is of Archangel Michael. This icon adds more complexity than the two previous ions. It requires painting wings, staff, hands, and adding a halo. Each level of complexity adds new techniques. The layering on the wings and halo are important new levels of complexity. Adding a halo takes practice to get the desired precision Maria achieves.

Using the same principles as before: start by tracing the icon image. Because the robe is white, it is necessary to trace more of the lines than is typical. Remember when tracing the eyes to just trace one line above and below.

Next is the application of glue for the gold leaf. Follow the same steps as done for the previous icons. This time there is glue above his head, wings, and below his wings.

Above (top to bottom): Photos of Maria's icon of Archangel Michael and glue applied for gold leaf.

Left: Gold leaf applied to the icon board.

THE HALO

This icon has a halo and we wanted the complete halo to fit onto the icon board. To do this, use a protractor to find the center point of the head. Maria did this before the gold leaf was applied. Once she marked the middle point, gold leaf was applied. She then marked again the middle point to make sure it was correct. I watched her do this and will practice on practice boards before attempting on an icon.

The next part was amazing to watch. Practice this technique before applying to an icon. Using a paintbrush, she added red paint to the drawing side of the protractor. Once the paint was applied, the halo was made using the protractor in one smooth movement.

Right: Using the protractor to find the middle point before and after the gold leaf is applied. Below: Adding paint to the end of the protractor (bottom left) and drawing the halo (bottom right).

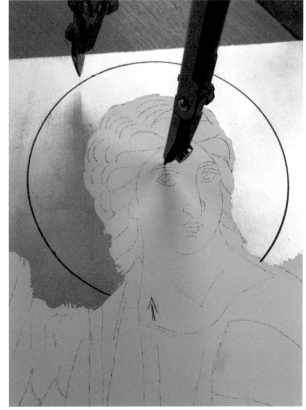

THE WINGS

Base of Wings

Red base color: red (rust) + orange + ochre. For the wings, we first painted the base color for the top and bottom. No additional egg is added to the paint. There are only a few layers on the wings, so make sure the base is covered completely and opaque.

Teal base color: blue + green. Paint the bottom wings using dark teal.

The Lines

Red lines: red base color + dark red (rust). This makes a darker shade of red for the red lines. Paint the lines on the wings. Maria painted the wings free hand to demonstrate the process. For the darker tips of the wings, use the line color mixed with egg. This adds shadow to the bottom of the wings.

Teal Lines: blue + green (slightly darker than the base). For the darker tips of the wings, use the line color mixed with egg.

Lower Wings

1st layer of light blue wings: base color + white + a little blue. Start by adding the first layer of light to the top part of the lower wings. This is done by painting a line on each side of the feather, then adding lines on the inside. There is also a rounded line that follows the upper wing. See the image to the right.

2nd layer of light: 1st layer of light + white. Thin lines are applied once again. The third layer of light is added on the upper part of the lower wing. The color is the *2nd light layer + additional white.* The top of the line is thicker and it tapers to very thin at the bottom.

Right (top to bottom): Base colors, red lines and shadow, colors mixed directly on glass surface, and light layers on blue wings.

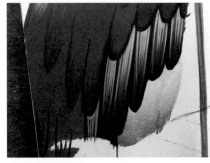

 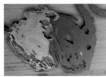

Upper Wings

The upper wings are painted with yellow-gold to add definition. The color is *gold ochre + yellow (light) + a little white*. The top of the lines are thicker, tapering at the bottom. Maria painted these lines. A second coat of paint is needed for the yellow. I applied the second coat of pain, but soon realized that I tended to add a slight curve at the very bottom. The best is to practice to make sure and make smooth lines that taper straight without curving. A zero, long bristled, brush is used for the fine lines of the wings.

Above: Yellow used for the lines on the wings. Left: Lines Maria painted on the wings. Two layers are needed (as can be seen by the darker yellow areas).

THE WALL

Wall base color: blue + red + white. The entire wall surface is painted with the base color. Two coats or more are necessary.

Wall lines: base color + more blue. As can be seen with the paint mixing palette above and to the right, Maria keeps the previous colors ready in case they are needed. These colors you see are the yellow, red, and orange from the wing and staff, and

Above: Mixing palette with colors for the staff, wings, and wall. Glass working surface. Right: Wall and robe base layer, lines, and 1st layer of light.

the purple from wall base color. This way if any touch up is necessary it can easily be done. After the base color, Maria mixed the line color and layers of light colors directly on the glass surface. The wall can be seen on the bottom of the above image.

1st layer of light: base color + white. The area is small, so mixing directly on the glass surface worked for ease and efficiency. Maria continued to mix the paint for the light layers directly on the glass surface. See the above image. The yellow is from the lines on the wings and the purple tones are the wall colors. Maria did this section and worked fast and free hand, meaning no tracing was necessary.

2nd layer of light: 1st light + more white. The paint for the final layer of light was mixed directly on the glass surface. Once the layers are added, the final step is to use only egg over the entire surface to blend the colors.

THE ROBE

Base color: white + ochre + a little dark red. Apply base color until solidly covered. Use smooth brush strokes and make sure to cover the entire area.

The robe lines: the base color + blue. This is a cooler color than the warm base color used for the robe. This highlights the contrast and provides added dimension. Apply the lines to the robe. The lines need to be applied in long, smooth strokes. The base color is then mixed with a little of the line color and egg to add shadow. This is used only in the lowest light areas (see image to the right). Also, it is only a small area, so the focus must remain on building the light layers, but adding some shadow helps add a bit of dimension. It is similar to the process used on the wings.

1st layer of light: base color + white. For the first layer of light, cover more of the area. Start by following the lines and then cover the areas with most light. With this light layer, most of the area is covered, except for the areas with shadow.

2nd layer of light: base + white + yellow. The second light layer requires smooth long lines, but do not cover all of the area: only apply this color to the areas with the most light. Always imagine where the next light layer will be applied.

3rd layer of light: 2nd light + yellow + white. The third layer of light is now applied. The full color is used for the highest light areas and then mixed with egg for the lower

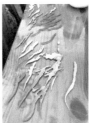

Above: Robe base color with added shadow and 1st layer of light. Mixing palette for robe and glass working surface

light areas. The egg helps to blend the layers. Be sure to use distinct, strong lines where necessary. The areas with the most light have clear distinct lines. Maria keeps the colors in the mixing palette, so any blending that is necessary can be done while working.

4th layer of light: 3rd light + more white. Now full color is used for the highest light areas. The rest is mixed with egg to blend with the other light layers. Thin lines are used in a crossing pattern when necessary. An image of the robe with the final layer is shown on page 66.

ARM BAND AND STAFF

The base: red + orange + ochre. Apply the red color to the entire area of the arm band and staff. For the staff, use the support tool to help draw the line straight. Typically three coats of paint are needed, resulting in a solid color with no white showing.

Lines: red + dark red. Paint the lines around the arm band and then draw one line down the staff. Two layers may be necessary.

1st layer of light: yellow + gold ochre. This layer is the only light layer, so apply in the areas where light is needed. Long, strong lines are used to give definition and highlights.

Above: Details of arm band and crossing patterns for completed robe. Top right: Robe with 3rd light layer and staff with base paint layer. Bottom right: Finished robe with the 4th light layer. Completed staff and arm band.

THE FACE AND HANDS

The base: dark red + a little light red + fresco green + ochre + cadmium yellow. Paint the hands, arms, and face using the base color. Three or four layers may be needed, resulting in a solid color with no white showing. Once dry, use the tracing paper to copy the lines of the icon. With a round tipped tool, lightly trace the face lines and lines on the hands.

The lines of the face, hands and hair: dark red + a little black. Paint the lines on the face. Do NOT paint the upper lip line, nor the middle neck line. Paint only the main lines of the eyes, eyebrows, nose, lower lip, middle lip, and chin. The lines around the hairline and face are also painted as well as the arms and hands. Take the time to correct any tracing mistakes that may have occurred. Fill in the eyes and eyebrows. Paint the hair with the brown from the line color. Once again this will be a solid color, so two or three layers may be necessary.

1st layer of light: cadmium red + yellow + gold ochre. This icon is different than the previous two. Hands and wings were not painted in the previous icons. Additionally, the face is much smaller. Maria demonstrated the first light layer. I started and then,

Above: Face lines and hair painted with face line color.

as we got further into the process, she took over and demonstrated the techniques to show how to add more dimension to the face and hands.

From a beginner's perspective, the creation of icons is really about learning how to see in a different way. The light layers are applied, and thus the shadow is created by the light. It is an opposite way of thinking for many and requires practice looking at things from a new perspective, and practice working with colors and layering with crossing brushstroke lines. I was mesmerized watching Maria paint.

I started the first light layer with lines below the eye, ear, forehead, and cheeks. Maria then expanded and showed a slightly different technique. She mixed a bit of red to the base color and light layer color and applied a small amount to the cheeks and forehead to create depth and definition.

Probably the most challenging part for me is knowing how far to paint the light layer. I always have to remember that the shadow is not covered, except with maybe a bit of egg near the edges. I have to imagine what the new light layer will look like on top of the current layer and paint accordingly. As shown in the images of Archangel Michael's face, Maria again added a bit more red to the cheeks and right side of the forehead. The red added more dimension and tone difference in the face. She did this by mixing directly on the glass table, matching the icon we were copying. As the lines move away from the most light areas, egg was mixed with paint and used alone to blend the colors.

Above: Glass surface used to mix paints for the face and hands. Right: 1st layer of light for the hands and face. A small amount of red was added for highlights on the cheek and forehead.

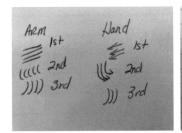

Above: Directional lines used for the arm and hand shown in the order they are applied. Right: Close up photo of the first layer of light on the hands and arm.

The hands do not have as much dimension as the face, so a slightly different process is used. Fewer crossing lines are used than on the face. First, it is important to paint the directional line with the most light: this is applied following the line patterns for 1st, 2nd, and 3rd, as shown in the above image. Using crossing lines, more definition and contour is created. This is done with the color plus egg.

2nd layer of light: orange + red + gold ochre + yellow cadmium. The second layer of light must cover nearly the entire surface of the 1st layer of light. Each layer is built upon the first, so the blending must be smooth. The color is mixed with the usual amount of egg. Then, use a dab of water, egg, and color to start the layer. Moving out of the areas with the highest light, more egg will be added. On the very edges, only egg is used. There needs to be contrast between the various light layers. Multidirectional lines are used to paint the face in a crossing pattern, as previously explained. A small amount of red was added for the cheek and heavy shadow areas to add more contrast.

3rd layer of light: 2nd light layer + yellow + gold ochre + a little orange. Each layer again builds on the previous layer. The key is to make sure to apply enough light with each color. This

Above and right: 3rd light layer on hands and face.

one has about three or four layers using a crossing pattern. Often the last layer is mainly egg or only egg to blend the colors.

4th layer of light: yellow + gold ochre. The same process is followed for the 4th light layer. Mix a dab of water, egg, and color on the glass table for the first layer. It needs to be applied similarly to the previous light

Below and right: 4th light layer.

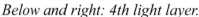

layers and may take up to three or four layers or more. We started by putting more light under the eye with one curved line following the eye and then short thin lines on the cheek.

How many layers of each light layer really depends on the degree of light needed. The light needs to be bright enough that when the white light layer is added, it is not too big of a contrast to the previous layer. Full color is added to the highest light areas. Then use egg mixed with color farther towards the shadow and eventually only egg to blend the layers. Use smooth, light lines to build the color. Make sure to continue to use crossing patterns. The lines will be shorter as the light layers progress.

5th layer of light: 4th light + white. The 5th light layer is applied by putting some of the color on the glass table, adding a dab of water, and a few drops of egg. Mix and then apply to the highest light areas. Use more egg and then only egg toward the lower light areas. Again, this needs to be applied with enough light so that when pure white is added, it is not too big of a contrast. Several layers need to be applied. Small brush strokes are used where there is the most light, and then thin lines are applied in a crossing pattern. Longer lines are painted with only egg to blend the colors. Compare color differences for the first application of the 5th layer of light and also once it is completed.

Below (left): Starting to apply the 5th layer of light. Below (right): Complete 5th layer of light.

6th Light Layer: white. On the glass table, mix a paintbrush full of white paint with a dab of water and one drop of egg. If necessary, add a dab or two more of mixed white paint. Use the white and a #1 paintbrush to paint the lines on the face, neck, and hands. See the images that follow to demonstrate the number of lines in the various locations. After the lines have been painted, use a little white with more egg, to blend the white. Then use only egg to continue blending.

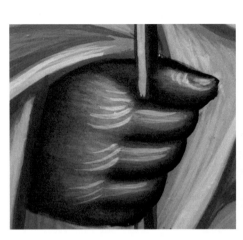

Above (left to right): White lines are painted on the hands and arm as shown. Right: White face lines are added. Typically two or three lines are painted. Pay special attention to the long line on the nose, below the right eye, and the neck lines.

Right and below: White lines blended with a bit of water and egg for final touches on the face and hands.

LINES

The lines on the face, hands, hair, and eyes involve the steps similar to the previous icons.

1. *Brownish red lines: red + black.* Use dark brown for the lines of the nose, bottom of lip and middle lip line, below the chin, around the eyes, and eyebrows. Mix egg with the color to fill in the eyebrows.

2. *Black lines: black.* Black is used for the upper line of the eyes and the pupil.

3. *Darker brown: 1st line color (brownish red) + black.* Is used for around the iris of the eye, one line on the bottom of the eyebrow, around the hair, and the hair lines.

Above: Eyes, lines, and lips. Below: Close-up photo of eyes and lips.

THE LIPS

Red. Red is used for the bottom and upper lips. Allow to dry, then use white mixed with red for the bottom lip. Mixing the paint with extra egg helps to soften the color of the bottom lip.

THE EYES

Pupil and Iris

Iris: Brown + black. Use the line color to go around the outside of the iris. *Black* is used for the pupil. Then use *red* with egg on the iris. *Orange + yellow* is then mixed and added to the iris. Next use brown with egg on the iris, then only yellow. On top of this, use brown with egg.

Whites of the Eyes

1. *Blue + white + extra egg.* Fill in more heavily the right side of the eye, then move below and to the left. This is the same for both eyes. When painting farther to the left, add more egg to the paint.

2. *White + a little blue.* Do the same, but cover less area with the full whitish blue color and use egg to blend on the outside and to the left. The strongest color is on the right. Paint over the area with egg to blend the colors.

3. *White.* Paint the right side, just a little more than a line, next to the right side of the iris. Use egg to then paint the rest and blend the colors. The same is done for both eyes. Look at the eyes from a distance and up close to see if they are correct. Continue to use the white with egg until it is the desired brightness.

Right: Close-up photo of whites of eyes, lips, and starting application of red for hair.

THE HAIR

The hair is painted using three layers of light. The layers of light are applied after the base brown color and the lines have dried. Use the following steps to complete the hair:

1. *Deep red: bright red + brown from lines + dark red.* Paint almost the full area inside of the lines. See images on this page. It is important to leave some of the base color visible through the red.

2. *Bright orange: yellow + orange.* Add two to three lines depending upon the size of the area. The third line will be very thin (see image on page 77).

3. *Bright yellow: yellow + gold ochre.* Paint small lines on top of the orange color (see image on page 77). Allow some of the previous two layers to be seen around the yellow lines. Add additional layers for brighter color.

Top right: Deep red added to the hair, please note the base color is partially visible. Right: Deep red applied to the hair. Lines are still visible as well as some of the base color.

THE GLORY, NAMING, AND SIGNING

Maria painted the Glory free hand. The Glory is the ribbon shown here on Archangel Michael and the top, center of the robe on Mary. The Glory was painted with a light purple made with *blue + red + white*. The first layer must dry before painting the second layer. Because it is over gold, a few layers will be necessary. She then painted the highlights with *white + a little blue*. Again, a few layers were needed. Finally, Maria mixed *blue + black* for the lines. Each layer needs to dry and then repeat for the desired color density.

Adding the name to the icon is done in red. This was first written with pencil and then painted with a few layers of red. Signing is done with white. The final touch is the framing with what we decided would be blue. The framing paint is colored acrylic paint with added pigment for the desired color. It surrounds the entire icon on all sides and also on the sides of the boards (bottom line only is shown in the above image).

Above and below: Finished hair, icon name, and glory.

Below: Archangel Michael icon named and signed.

CHAPTER 6
BASIC SUPPLIES

BOARDS

Handmade Boards (cut to size and sanded)
Glues (two types as mentioned)
Cotton
Gesso (handmade or white acrylic)
Sandpaper grit: 120, 150, 180, 220, 320, 400
Sanding hand tool
Alcohol

GOLD LEAF

Gold leaf (22 or 23-karat gold)
Fine Glue
Glue
Shellac

PAINTING SUPPLIES

Pigments (basic colors are listed on pages 81 and 82)
Egg, Water, & Vinegar
Paintbrushes for painting (natural bristle brushes)
• sizes: 00, 0, 1, and long tipped 1, 2, 4, 6, 8 (others of
  personal choice)
Paintbrushes for mixing. Only use these for mixing paint.
Paintbrushes for glue
• Typically flat, wider brush for smooth strokes
Varnish
Acrylic paint for framing around edges

Above: Top of bracing tool with soft end. Below: Bracing tool must be long enough to reach across painting easel and with very soft velvet fabric on the end so it won't leave marks on the icon.

ADDITIONAL ITEMS

Tracing paper
Carbon paper for transferring
Round tipped tool
Protractor, ruler
Long bracing tool

Right: Tracing paper and round tipped tool for tracing.

PIGMENTS

Right: Pigments with names. Below: Pigments Maria uses for her icons. Please note that due to color changes with printing the colors may not be an exact match. They may appear darker in the images than when viewed in person.

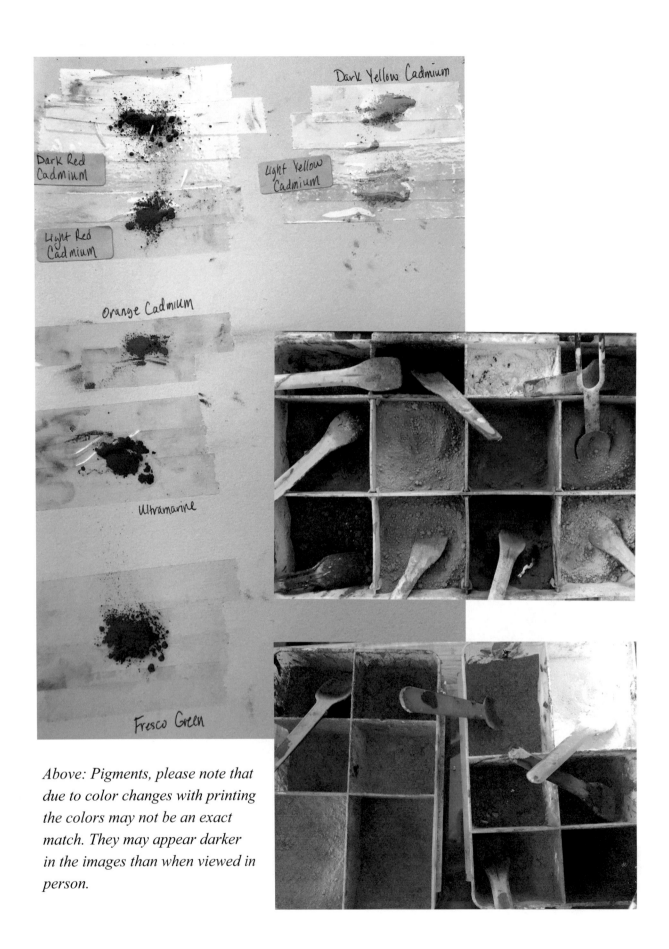

Dark Yellow Cadmium

Dark Red Cadmium

Light Yellow Cadmium

Light Red Cadmium

Orange Cadmium

Ultramarine

Fresco Green

Above: Pigments, please note that due to color changes with printing the colors may not be an exact match. They may appear darker in the images than when viewed in person.

TEMPLATES

The template shown here and on pages 84 and 85 are icons Maria painted. The image of Christ is cropped to show more details of the face. Please remember to sign, apply a border, and extend the robe as desired.

84

AFTERWORD

COLETTE MARIA EVANS

I grew up in Pocatello, Idaho, USA. I have always loved art, from the time I was a little girl, creating with pastels and convincing family members to buy them for 5 to 10 cents apiece, to when I more seriously learned oil painting as an adult. Art has always played a role in my life, either by my appreciation of art or my own experimenting with color, texture, and creation.

Pursuing my Ph.D. in Health Education, teaching, and starting my own business, Inspire LLC, have left little room to pursue art further, as I would wish. My professional career has focused on facilitating inspirational and health promotion workshops for teens and adults. This pursuit and my family have taken me to amazing places around the world. Therefore I have been fortunate to have seen first hand some of the most profound icons in existence.

I currently live with my family in Hailey, Idaho, USA. It is with great appreciation and gratitude that I have had the unique opportunity for this extended stay in Patmos, Dodecanese, Greece, to study iconography with Maria Pente. What a pleasure it has been to learn from her. I have much to learn, and need lots of practice, but now I have some of the basics to continue on this journey of iconography. It is our hope that this serves as a "tips of the trade" guide for those pursuing iconography. I hope you can visit Maria in Patmos to watch her create and see her work first hand.

Above: Colette in Maria's studio Patmos, Greece.

Above: Icon of John the Baptist painted by Colette during her most recent trip to Patmos to study with Maria. This icon involved more complexity and new techniques demonstrated by Maria.

Made in United States
Troutdale, OR
07/13/2023